Contents

Some words are shown in bold, **like this**. You can find out what they mean by looking in the Glossary.

The Moon landing

One small step

At 9.32 a.m. on 16 July 1969, *Apollo 11* began an epic journey from the Kennedy Space Center, Florida, USA. In just 11 minutes the spacecraft pushed free of Earth's **gravity** and went into **orbit**. It circled the Earth one and a half times before its powerful thrusters burst into life and sent it out of orbit and across space. The three astronauts on board *Apollo 11* were Michael Collins, Neil Armstrong, and Edwin "Buzz" Aldrin. They had a mission that no one had ever been given before. They were to cross 386,160 kilometres (240,000 miles) of space and land on the Earth's moon.

Four days later, on 20 July, Armstrong and Aldrin climbed into the **lunar module** *Eagle*, which then separated from the **command module** *Columbia* and began edging towards the moon's surface. At 4.18 p.m. came the message, "The *Eagle* has landed". For the first time, there were people on the Moon.

The Moon – people have wondered about it ever since they first walked on Earth. Then, in 1969, two men had the thrill of crossing space and walking on its surface.

TURNING POINTS IN HISTORY

Revised and Updated

The Moon Landing

The Race into Space

www.heinemann.co.uk/library
Visit our website to find out more information about **Heinemann Library** books.

To order:
☎ Phone 44 (0) 1865 888112
🖹 Send a fax to 44 (0) 1865 314091
🖳 Visit the Heinemann Bookshop at www.heinemann.co.uk/library to browse our catalogue and order online.

First published in Great Britain by
Heinemann Library,
Halley Court, Jordan Hill, Oxford OX2 8EJ,
part of Harcourt Education.
Heinemann is a registered trademark of
Harcourt Education Ltd.

Editorial: Clare Lewis
Designed by Tokay Interactive Ltd.
(www.tokay.co.uk)
Printed in China by WKT Company Limited

13 digit ISBN: 978 0 431 07713 0 (hb)
10 09 08 07 06
10 9 8 7 6 5 4 3 2 1

13 digit ISBN: 978 0 431 07777 2 (pb)
12 11 10 09 08
10 9 8 7 6 5 4 3 2 1

British Library Cataloguing in Publication Data
Kelly, Nigel
Turning Points in History: The Moon Landing:
The Race into Space. – 2nd edition
629.4'5
A full catalogue record for this book is
available from the British Library.

Acknowledgements
The Publishers would like to thank the
following for permission to reproduce
photographs:
Boden, Gareth: p. **27**; Corbis: pp. **9**, **16**, **17**,
18, (Bettman) pp. **6**, **10**, **14**, (NASA) p. **23**,
(Roger Ressmeyer) p. **11**; Fortean Picture
Library: p. **13**; Mary Evans Picture Library:
p. **12**; NASA: pp. **5**, **7**, **23**, **24**, (Science
Photo Library) pp. **15**, **19**, **22**; Photodisc:
p **4**; Science & Society Picture Library: p. **8**;
Space Imaging Inc: p. **25**; Science Photo
Library/NASA: p. **28**.

Cover photograph reproduced with
permission of Nasa.

The publishers would like to thank Stewart
Ross for his help in the preparation of this
book.

Every effort has been made to contact
copyright holders of any material reproduced
in this book. Any omissions will be rectified
in subsequent printings if notice is given to
the Publisher.

One giant leap

More than six hours later, Armstrong and Aldrin emerged from the lunar module. As over 600 million people watched on their television sets back on Earth, Armstrong became the first man to walk on the moon. After taking his first step he declared:

"That's one small step for a man, one giant leap for mankind."

The US President, Richard Nixon, was so impressed by what Armstrong and Aldrin had done that he sent them a message saying,

"...because of what you have done, the heavens have become a part of man's world."

The astronauts had several tasks to perform. They collected nearly 22 kilograms (50 pounds) of soil samples to take back to Earth, set up a solar wind experiment and, of course, took photographs of each other as souvenirs! They also erected an American flag. After spending 2 hours and 31 minutes on the Moon, the astronauts returned to the lunar module to prepare to return to *Apollo 11*.

Buzz Aldrin on the Moon. Neil Armstrong and the lunar module can be seen reflected in Aldrin's visor.

Apollo 11 : We're coming home

Once they were back inside the lunar module, Armstrong and Aldrin removed their spacesuits and rested for several hours. Then came the heart-stopping moment when it was time to lift off and rejoin the command module. Fortunately it went without a hitch and the astronauts were soon safely aboard *Apollo 11*, orbiting the Moon. The return journey took four days, with the astronauts finally splashing down in the sea 1,300 kilometres (800 miles) from Hawaii, on 24 July.

A turning point?

In 1969 the *Apollo 11* mission caused great excitement. Scientists declared that we had entered a new era in space exploration. The last great barrier in exploration had been broken down. We were now "in space" and there was no looking back. However, things have not worked out quite as the scientists expected. It has now been over 35 years since people have visited the Moon. The dream of setting up colonies of people living on the Moon or in space cities has remained just a dream. So was the *Apollo 11* mission really a turning point in our history – or just a very exciting part of it?

The Moon landing made front-page headlines in newspapers in the United States and all over the world.

What if it had gone wrong?

We now know that if the lunar module had failed to take off to rejoin *Columbia*, Armstrong and Aldrin would have been left on the Moon, either to die slowly or to commit suicide. A plan was drawn up in which US President Richard Nixon would telephone their wives to express his condolences before going on television to inform the world that "There is a corner of another world that is forever mankind."

Neil Armstrong, the first man to set foot on the moon

Neil Armstrong – first man on the Moon

Neil Armstrong was born in Ohio in the United States in 1930. From 1949 he served as a pilot in the US Navy and fought in the Korean War (1950–53). He later became a test pilot, and in 1962 joined the astronaut training programme. His first flight into space was in 1966 when he was command pilot on *Gemini 8*. Although his became one of the most famous names in history when he walked on the Moon, he did not stay in the space programme. In 1971 he became Professor of Aerospace Engineering at a US university and in 1980 took up a career in business.

From balloons to rockets

The dream of flight

Apollo 11 had taken men to the Moon and back but the idea that humans could fly had been no more than a dream until the late 18th century.

Hot-air balloons

In September 1783 two French brothers, Joseph and Etienne Montgolfier, launched a balloon powered by hot air created by burning straw, wool, old shoes, and rotting meat. The smell was terrible, but there were no complaints from the balloon's passengers – a sheep, a duck, and a cockerel. All three survived the experience, and manned flights soon became common.

Enter the aeroplane

The next breakthrough in flight technology came in 1903, in Dayton, Ohio, USA. Wilbur and Orville Wright succeeded in flying an aeroplane with a petrol-driven engine. The flight lasted just 12 seconds, but the age of flight had begun. Another important advance came when Sir Frank Whittle invented the **jet engine** in the United Kingdom, in 1941. Aircraft could now travel at much greater speeds. In 1947 the American Bell X-1 became the first aircraft to fly faster than the speed of sound. Five years later the world's first jet-airliner, the British De Haviland Comet, went into service.

The Montgolfier hot-air balloon took people into the air for the first time on 21 November 1783.

War in the air

The first use to which people put this new technology was to help them fight wars. A few aircraft carried out bombing raids during World War I. By World War II, aircraft bombers were used with devastating results. On 6 August 1945, the first **atomic bomb** was dropped from a US B-29 bomber on the Japanese city of Hiroshima. It killed 80,000 men, women, and children outright, and many more died later from radiation sickness caused by the bomb.

Rocket technology

Meanwhile scientists were developing the technology that would make war in the air even more deadly. In 1926 Robert Goddard, an American scientist, built the first effective **rocket**. By 1939 the German rocket engineer Wernher von Braun had succeeded in developing rockets that could replace the German flying bombs. These V2 rockets could reach an altitude of 80 kilometres (50 miles) before falling and exploding. Not long afterwards rockets began to travel fast enough to escape the pull of the Earth's gravity and travel into space for the first time!

This Trident inter-continental ballistic missile was launched from a nuclear-powered submarine by the US Navy as part of a demonstration during the Cold War.

The Cold War

After World War II, a **Cold War** developed between the Western countries, led by the United States, and the countries of Eastern Europe, led by the **Soviet Union**. The West was **democratic**, while the East was **communist**. Each side was determined to prove that its system was best. The two sides spent huge sums of money building up supplies of weapons, although no direct fighting actually took place. Both sides used rocket technology to develop weapons. **ICBMs** (Inter-Continental Ballistic Missiles) were rockets with **nuclear bombs** attached that could hit targets several thousand kilometres away.

The final frontier: into the unknown

The space race

The desire to win the Cold War pushed both the United States and the Soviet Union to develop the technology to send rockets into space. What better way could there be to prove the superiority of your country than to be first to put a man in space – or better still, on the Moon? So, from the mid-1950s the two **superpowers** took part in a "space race". Winning this race would show how much more advanced the victor's science and technology were than that of their rivals.

The race begins

In August 1957 Soviet scientists had developed a rocket to power their ICBMs. The same type of rocket was used to send a **satellite** into space on 4 October 1957. *Sputnik 1* was a tiny sphere, housing two radio transmitters, but its trip around the Earth marked the beginning of the space age. In November 1957 the larger *Sputnik 2* carried a dog, Laika, into space. She died of heat exhaustion before her air ran out.

Wernher von Braun, the rocket engineer who played an important part in developing rockets used in space exploration.

The success of the *Sputnik* launches made the Americans even more determined to launch their own rockets. Their first attempt, in December 1957, ended in failure when the launch rocket exploded shortly after lift-off. In January 1958, however, they were successful when *Explorer 1* was launched into space by a *Jupiter* rocket – developed by Wernher von Braun, who had moved to the United States after World War II.

In 1959 the United States sent monkeys into space. In contrast to the *Sputnik 2* mission, the animals were brought safely back to Earth. The technology existed to send animals into space and bring them back. Now it was time to do it with humans.

Miss Baker, one of the "monkeynauts" sent into space by the United States in 1959.

Wernher von Braun (1912–77)

Wernher von Braun came from a wealthy German family. He became interested in astronomy when his mother gave him a telescope as a present. It is said that he did badly in maths and physics at school until he was given a copy of a book about rockets. He was so annoyed that he could not understand it that he began to work really hard.

In 1930 he joined the German Society for Space Travel and by 1934 had helped develop a rocket that could reach a height of 2.4 kilometres (1.5 miles). Although he helped work on developing the V2 flying bomb, von Braun did not approve of the military use of the rocket. He surrendered to the United States in 1945 and began working on rocket development for them. He was mainly responsible for the development of the first American satellite (Explorer I) in 1958, and the Saturn rocket that took American astronauts to the Moon in 1969.

Destroying the myths

Ever since humans have walked on the Earth, they have stared up at space and wondered what is out there. By 1959, improved technology and the desire to win the Cold War had brought us to the point where we were about to send people into space. But what would we find there?

There are many interesting myths about what space is. For example, if you look closely at a full Moon it appears to have a face on it. This has led some superstitious people to believe in a "man in the Moon".

A 1930s story book showing invaders from Sirius trying to steal the Earth

The Martians have landed

Other equally fanciful ideas exist about other planets and stars. Many books and films have appeared in which Martians with deadly ray guns land on Earth and begin attacking "Earthlings". Perhaps the most famous was *War of the Worlds*, written in 1898 by H.G. Wells. It gives an account of Martians landing on Earth and capturing people to drink their blood. When the story was broadcast on US radio in the 1930s it caused widespread panic, as some people thought they were listening to a real account of a Martian invasion!

Is there anybody out there?

Some people are convinced that the unidentified flying objects (UFOs) seen in our skies are spaceships from other planets. Others try to explain man-made structures from our past by suggesting that there must have been help from outer space. How else could ancient peoples have built Stonehenge in the United Kingdom, or the cliff settlements at Mesa Verde in Colorado, USA? Those who think Earth has been visited from afar point to evidence such as cave drawings that seem to have astronauts in them. Is there a simple explanation for this?

So far our explorations into space have produced no evidence of life on other planets. Perhaps one day they will, but there is one thing of which we can be fairly sure. If we ever do find life in space it will not look like a strange human being, carrying a deadly ray gun, nor is it likely to say, "May the force be with you"!

A prehistoric painting from an Italian cave. Does it show that our ancestors were visited by people in helmets with antennae?

Martians, as described by H.G. Wells in *War of the Worlds*

"They had huge round bodies — or rather heads — about four feet in diameter, each body having in front of it a face. This face had no nostrils — indeed the Martians do not seem to have had any sense of smell — but it had a pair of very large, dark coloured eyes, and just beneath this, a kind of fleshy beak. In a group around the mouth were 16, slender, almost whip-like tentacles, arranged in two bunches of eight each."

Men on the Moon

From the late 1950s onwards, the United States and the Soviet Union worked tirelessly to be the first to put men into space. On 12 April 1961, those working on the US space programme heard the news they had been dreading. The Soviet Union had launched a manned flight. Yuri Gagarin became the first person in space. His cry of "We're off!" as his rocket took off became as famous in the Soviet Union as did Neil Armstrong's later words in the United States. Gagarin, the son of a carpenter, became a great Soviet hero.

The US President, John F. Kennedy, sent a message of congratulations to the Soviet leader, Nikita Khrushchev, but really he was disappointed and felt his nation had been humiliated. He was determined that the United States would be first to achieve the next big goal in space – landing men on the Moon. A few weeks after Gagarin's flight, Kennedy made a speech in which he said, "I believe that this nation should commit itself to achieving the goal, before this decade is out, of landing a man on the Moon and returning him safely to Earth."

Yuri Gagarin was the first man in space. In April 1961 he spent 1 hour 48 minutes orbiting Earth at a maximum speed of 27,000 kph (17,000 mph) – about 10 times faster than a rifle bullet flies!

Into orbit

In February 1962, John Glenn became the first American to orbit the Earth. For the next seven years the space race continued. When the Soviets carried out a **spacewalk** in March 1965, the United States followed three months later. When the Soviets landed an unmanned spacecraft on the Moon in February 1966, the United States was just four months behind.

But it was the United States that finally won the race in July 1969 when Armstrong, Aldrin, and Collins set off on their famous voyage. The world watched on television as mankind finally conquered the last frontier. We had reached the Moon.

The launch of *Saturn V,* the rocket that carried *Apollo 11* into space.

Sending *Apollo* to the Moon

The rocket that sent *Apollo* was called *Saturn V*. It was over 110 metres (360 feet) high and weighed more than 3,000 tonnes, although most of this was fuel. The rocket was made up of three "stages."

- **Stage 1:** Fired for 2.5 minutes and enabled the rocket to reach a speed of 9,000 kph (almost 6,000 mph). At 60 km (37 miles) this stage fell away into the ocean.

- **Stage 2:** The rocket was much lighter. When the Stage 2 rockets fired for six minutes *Saturn* reached a speed of 25,000 kph (about 15,500 mph). At 180 km (112 miles) Stage 2 dropped away.

- **Stage 3:** These rockets fired for two minutes to reach a speed of 28,000 kph (17,400 mph) – any less and gravity would have brought *Saturn* back to Earth. After orbiting Earth, *Saturn's* rockets fired again for five minutes and sent *Apollo* across space to the Moon at a speed of 40,000 kph (25,000 mph).

Exploring the Moon

Neil Armstrong and Buzz Aldrin are the most famous men to have set foot on the Moon, but they are not the only ones. Between 1969 and 1972 five more *Apollo* spacecraft made the journey to the Moon successfully, and 12 men walked on its surface – all of them American.

Why go back?

When the United States landed the first men on the Moon, they had won the space race. Surely that was enough. Why did they go back for another 20 *Apollo* missions? The technology, money, and plans were still in place, and the astronauts wanted to go, but the most important reason was science. The *Apollo 11* astronauts had brought some soil and rock samples back with them, but scientists needed more information to answer questions such as how and when had the Moon been formed?

On the Moon

The five *Apollo* missions that followed *Apollo 11* all landed at different sites on the Moon. Astronauts explored and mapped the Moon's mountains, valleys, and plains, although the *Apollo 14* men almost got lost in the unfamiliar landscape. Astronauts set up automatic scientific stations, and brought over 385 kilograms (850 pounds) of soil and rock samples back to Earth. On the last mission, *Apollo 17*, astronauts camped out on the Moon for three days.

On the last three missions, the astronauts drove around the Moon in a battery-powered car called the *Lunar Rover*. It allowed them to travel much further and explore more rugged terrain.

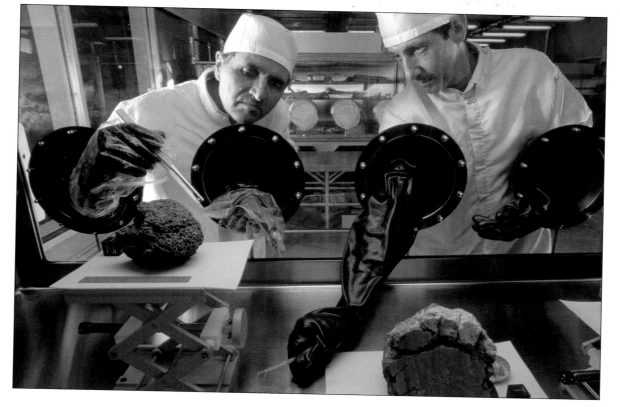

Why stop?

The main reason America stopped sending men to the Moon was cost. Some people thought that the $25 billion cost of the *Apollo* Project might have been better spent on other things. When *Apollo 17* took off from the Moon's surface on 13 December 1972, human beings said goodbye to their closest neighbour for the last time in the 20th century. They left a plaque behind them that said, "Here man completed his first exploration of the Moon." When, if ever, will people return?

What did they find out?

The scientists who studied the Moon rock made some exciting discoveries. They found out that the Moon is over four billion years old – about the same age as the Earth. We still do not know for certain how the Moon was formed, but many scientists believe that a huge lump of rock about the size of Mars crashed into the Earth over four billion years ago. This collision sent a large chunk – about one-sixth – of the newly formed Earth flying off into space. The debris from the collision started to orbit the Earth, and gradually joined together to form the Moon. The crash left a huge hole in the Earth's surface that is still visible today – the basin of the Pacific Ocean.

Danger!

The journey into space is incredibly dangerous. At the moment of lift-off, astronauts are surrounded by thousands of tonnes of highly explosive rocket fuel. Once the astronauts are out in space they have to hope that the engineers and scientists have got everything right. If any piece of the highly advanced technology fails, there is no breakdown organization to come and rescue them! Fortunately, most space missions are completed without a hitch, but both the United States and the Soviet Union have had fatal accidents.

Lost in space

In 1967, a month after their *Apollo 1* was due to take off, three American astronauts were killed when a spark in their cabin set fire to their spacecraft during a practice session on the launch pad.

In the same year, a Soviet **cosmonaut** died at the end of his space mission when his *Soyuz 1* spacecraft plunged to the ground in a field near Orenberg, in Russia. The parachute, which should have acted as a brake to slow the spacecraft down, had become tangled.

In 1971 the three-man crew of the Soviet *Soyuz 11* was killed when a valve failed during their **re-entry** into Earth's **atmosphere**. They were not wearing pressure suits and died as a result of **decompression sickness**. The rapid change in pressure meant that their blood literally boiled in their veins.

The *Challenger* space badge, with the "apple for the teacher", Christa McAuliffe

The *Challenger* disaster

The terrible *Challenger* accident occurred in 1986. The United States had developed a space "shuttle" that could be launched into space and then fly astronauts back to Earth, landing on an airstrip instead of ditching in the sea. Millions of people were watching as a huge rocket lifted the space shuttle *Challenger* towards Earth's **orbit**. On board were seven astronauts. For the first time, the crew included someone who was not a professional astronaut, the teacher Christa McAuliffe. She was to carry out experiments suggested by schoolchildren, and even hold some "live lessons" during the flight. To mark the event an "apple for the teacher" was included in the crew's space badge.

At lift-off a fault developed in one of the rocket boosters and, 73 seconds into the flight, *Challenger* exploded. Several weeks later the remains of *Challenger* were found in the Atlantic Ocean. Investigations showed that the crew had probably survived the explosion but had been killed when the shuttle hit the sea. Mercifully, they would have fainted only seconds after *Challenger* had begun its 18-kilometre (11-mile) plummet back to Earth.

The *Challenger* disaster was such a terrible shock that it was over two and a half years before shuttle flights started again. Humankind had received a terrible reminder of the dangers of space flight.

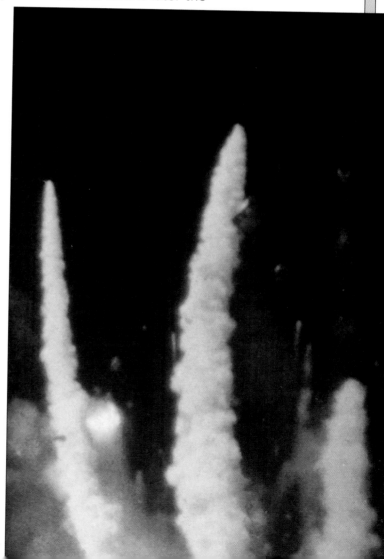

The explosion of the space shuttle *Challenger*,
73 seconds after take-off on 28 January 1986

Beyond the Moon

By 1981 people had made six visits to the Moon and developed a space shuttle that could be used over and over again. It seemed that humankind was near to conquering space. Steps were already under way to learn about the Universe far beyond. Long before *Apollo 11* reached the Moon, spacecraft had been sent deep into that universe. By the beginning of the 21st century, space **probes** had been launched towards every planet, the last mission leaving for Pluto in 2006.

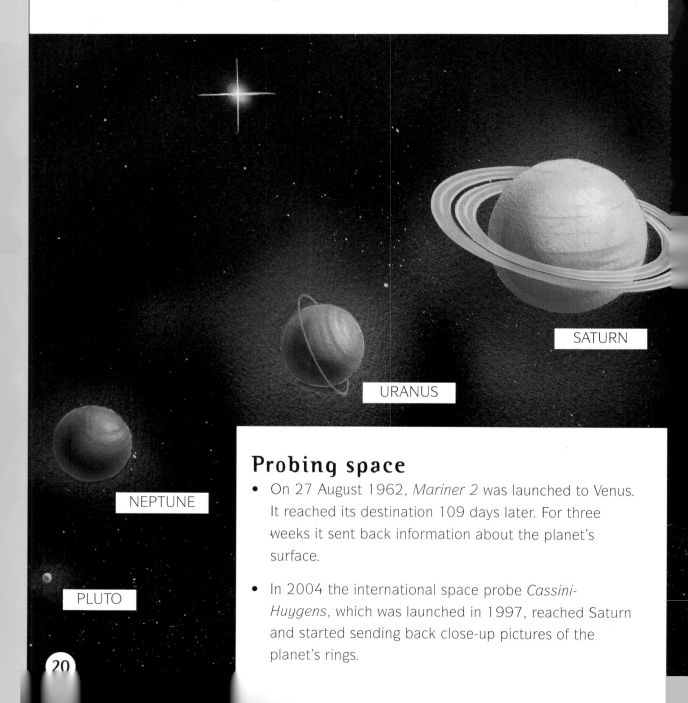

SATURN

URANUS

NEPTUNE

PLUTO

Probing space

- On 27 August 1962, *Mariner 2* was launched to Venus. It reached its destination 109 days later. For three weeks it sent back information about the planet's surface.

- In 2004 the international space probe *Cassini-Huygens*, which was launched in 1997, reached Saturn and started sending back close-up pictures of the planet's rings.

- In July 1965, *Mariner 4* sent back the first close-up pictures of Mars. By 1971, further missions had managed to map the whole of the planet's surface. In 1989, US President Bush set a target of landing on Mars by the year 2019.

- In February 2001 the Near Earth Asteroid Rendezvous (NEAR) spacecraft became the first to land on the surface of an asteroid (Eros).

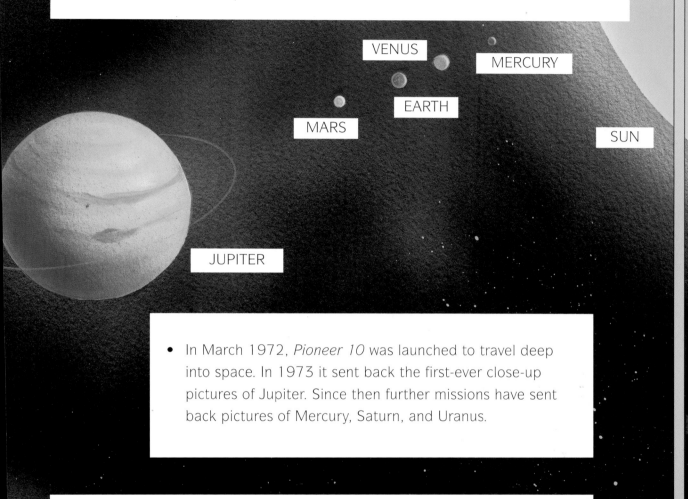

VENUS

MERCURY

EARTH

MARS

SUN

JUPITER

- In March 1972, *Pioneer 10* was launched to travel deep into space. In 1973 it sent back the first-ever close-up pictures of Jupiter. Since then further missions have sent back pictures of Mercury, Saturn, and Uranus.

Living in space

As our knowledge of our Universe increases, the day when humans live in space, or in colonies on other planets, gets closer. Both the United States and the Soviet Union have launched **space stations**, which can be used to test the effects on the human body of spending long periods in space. In 1986 the Soviet Union launched the space station *Mir*, and two astronauts stayed on it for a whole year.

In 2001, the International Space Station was launched. It is four times larger than the *Mir* space station.

Space facts

Take-off

Within four seconds of lift-off the space shuttle reaches 160 kilometres per hour (100 miles per hour). Within 40 seconds it is travelling at more than the speed of sound. The pressure that astronauts experience during this acceleration is about 10 times that felt by airline passengers during take-off. After 8.5 minutes the engines cut off as the shuttle leaves the Earth's atmosphere. Some astronauts cheer at this point, as the terrible pressure on their bodies is replaced by **weightlessness**.

An astronaut's spacesuit enables survival in the hostile environment outside the spacecraft.

During lift-off there is a danger that the shuttle might lose control. In case this happens, spacecraft are fitted with a flight termination system (FTS). If there was a danger that an out of control shuttle might threaten life on Earth, a member of the space team on the ground would send a signal and the craft would blow up. Inevitably, the crew would be killed.

A basic question

Astronauts complain that when they give interviews the question that everyone wants to ask is, "How do you go to the toilet in space?" Spacecraft do have toilets but, as water does not flow in space, they are flushed by air. It has been described as like "going to the bathroom in a vacuum cleaner". Solid waste is returned to Earth, but liquid waste is dumped in space. An astronaut recently described the "urine dump" as beautiful to watch because the fluid instantly turns into shiny ice crystals.

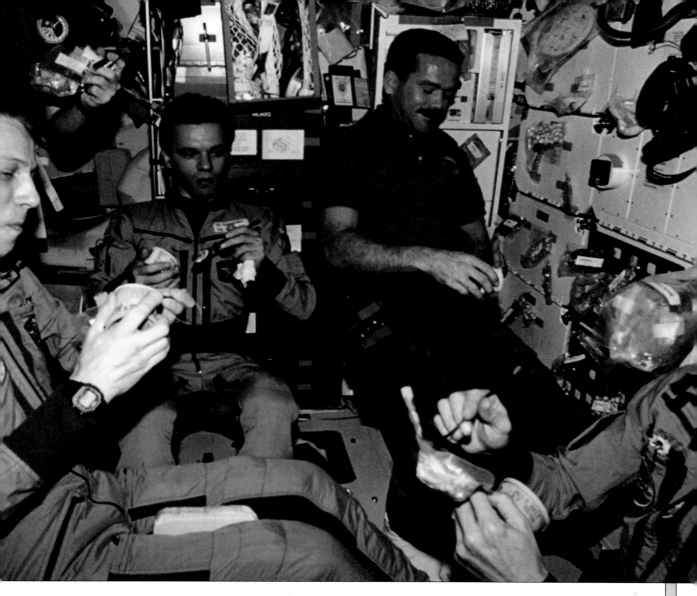

Astronauts eating in a weightless environment. The food packaging is designed to stop the food floating away from it.

Weightlessness

Once in space, there is no gravity and anything that is not tied down floats. If you cut yourself in this weightless environment the blood forms a perfectly spherical droplet and floats away like a tiny, scarlet balloon. Astronauts sleep in sleeping bags attached to the wall. This stops them banging into each other. It also means that when they go to sleep they can wake up in the same place.

Astronauts look fatter in space than on Earth, because more blood than usual goes to the head. If they lived in space for long periods they would get taller because there is no gravity to compact the bones. In a weightless environment, muscles do hardly any work. Exercise is important to stop these muscles wasting away.

What have we gained from the space race?

Space exploration is incredibly expensive; for example, between 1969 and 1972, the *Apollo* Project cost the United States over $25 billion. Some critics of space flight have suggested that the money would be better spent on fighting poverty or famine. When the Soviet Union broke up into its individual states in 1991, its space programme virtually came to an end because it was so expensive. So has it all been worth it?

Does it really cost so much?

The National Aeronautics and Space Administration (NASA), which runs the US space programme, argues that space exploration is not really expensive. It says that thousands of jobs have been created by the space race and that advances in technology brought about through space exploration have made US businesses more efficient and profitable. It calculates that, for every $1 spent on the space programme, America has become richer by $7, because of extra taxes paid by people working in it, or improvement in the economy. Whether or not NASA is correct, the space race has definitely brought enormous benefits.

NASA ground control, Houston, from where space flights are managed

Advances in science and technology

Scientists have had to overcome some very difficult problems to put people on the Moon.

- How do we get outside Earth's atmosphere?
- How do we stop spacecraft burning up on re-entry?
- How do we communicate with astronauts in space?
- How do we cope with weightlessness?

In finding solutions to these problems, the teams working on the space programme have vastly increased our knowledge of science and technology.

Satellite communications

These scientific and technological advances have brought enormous benefits for people in general, outside the space programme. Satellites in orbit above the Earth are used to relay television pictures, to speed up intercontinental telephone calls, and to provide valuable information about the Earth. Details of extreme weather (such as hurricanes) can be identified by satellites. The existence of a huge hole in the Earth's **ozone layer** over the Antarctic was confirmed by the satellite *Nimbus 7* in 1987. In 1999 the United States launched satellite *Ikonos* to provide pictures of the Earth that are so detailed that they can pick out objects on the ground as small as one metre (three feet) across.

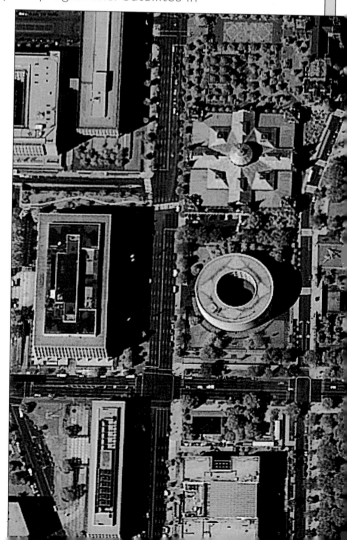

Buildings in New York City viewed from space. It is now possible to download images that have been sent from satellites onto any laptop computer within minutes.

Spin-offs

The increased scientific and technological developments needed to overcome the problems involved in space travel have produced **spin-offs** that have improved everyday life on Earth.

Medicine

One of the areas to see major benefits has been medicine. In 1990 the Hubble Space Telescope was launched to give better views of space. The same technology is now used to help doctors find cancer cells in sick people. As devices used in spacecraft have to be very small and light, many tiny instruments have become available to doctors and surgeons. For example, tiny cameras can now be inserted into patients' bodies to help with diagnosis. Hearing aids smaller than a human fingernail and voice-controlled wheelchairs have been developed because astronauts sometimes have to steer spacecraft by voice.

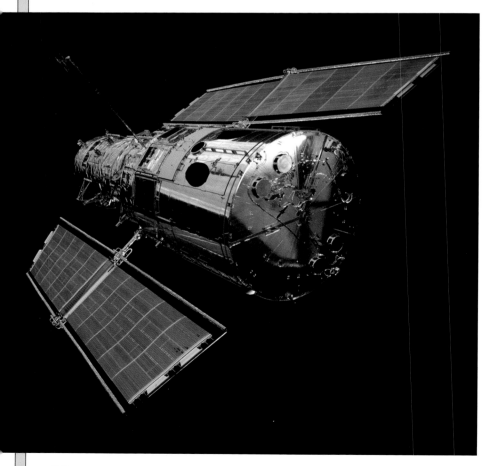

The Hubble Space Telescope, in orbit around the Earth at a height of 610 km (380 miles), has no crew. From outside the Earth's atmosphere, it takes images of space that are better than pictures produced through any land-based telescope.

There have been other valuable non-electronic spin-offs in medicine. The insulating material used for rocket fuel tanks can be used in hospitals to prevent bed sores. Aerospace engineers have also produced a special bed that enables patients with serious burns to lie more comfortably by floating on a cushion of air.

Daily life

Daily life has been affected by the space programme, perhaps more than anyone realizes. The need for small but powerful instruments on board spacecraft produced the silicon chip. These tiny electronic circuits are now used in the processors we find in everything from washing machines to laptops. Cars are designed by a computer program devised to design spaceships. Wristwatches run on tiny batteries designed to time devices in space.

Even training shoes are a product of the space programme. The need to develop moon boots, with cushioning and ventilation, has resulted in better footwear for athletes, which reduce fatigue and the chances of injury.

Space in the kitchen

Did you know that non-stick frying pans and casserole dishes that can go straight from the freezer to the oven, and then on to your table, are the result of the space programme? Spacecraft go through extremes of heat in space and materials had to be developed that could resist these temperatures. Now they are used to make your kitchenware!

The great debate

Overrated?

The Moon landing certainly was an important event. There are some, though, who claim that its significance has been exaggerated.

Question 1: Was the Moon landing really a turning point?

Yes!

- By getting human beings living and carrying out complicated operations in space, the Moon landing paved the way for all the really important operations that followed, such as the space shuttle programme.

- After the Moon landing the Soviet Union knew it had lost the space race. This lowered Soviet morale and the people's confidence in their government. This was an important step towards the collapse of the Soviet communism.

No!

- The real breakthrough was not the Moon landing but the first ventures into space – Sputnik I (1957) and the voyage of Yuri Gagarin (1961). Once these giant steps had been taken, the rest was inevitable.

- The importance of the Moon landing was exaggerated by the United States for propaganda purposes. That is why they showed it on TV. This helped show it as more of a triumph of capitalism and democracy than of technology.

What do you think?

An astronaut works in space on the construction of the International Space Station in 2004.

The right price?

Question 2: Was the Moon landing worth the cost?

Yes!

- It showed the world the supremacy of capitalism and democracy.

- It helped undermine Soviet communism and thus bring the Cold War to an end.

- It developed all kinds of technologies that were useful in other areas (see page 27).

- It boosted US industry and technology through massive government spending. As the US economy was by far the world's largest, everyone benefited indirectly.

No!

- It was done primarily to help the image of the politicians who voted to spend the money, not for the ordinary Americans who had to pay the taxes.

- Although there were technological spin-offs, these could have occurred more quickly and cheaply if money had been spent on them directly.

- The technological spin-offs would have occurred anyway.

- The vast sums spent on the space programme would have benefited the United States and the world in general if they had been spent on more useful things, such as health care, overseas aid, or better housing.

Many of these arguments, for and against, apply to space exploration in general. Where do you stand?

Find out more

Using the Internet

Explore the Internet to find out more about the moon landing and space exploration. You can use a search engine, such as www.yahooligans.com or www.google.com, and type in keywords or phrases such as *NASA*, *Neil Armstrong*, *space race*, or *space shuttle*.

More books to read

Mason, Paul. *Days That Shook the World: The Moon Landing.* (Hodder Children's Books, 2003)

Mist, Rosalind and Solway, Andrew. *Stargazer's Guides: Can We Travel to the Stars? Space Flight and Space Exploration.* (Heinemann Library, 2006)

Sheehan, Sean. *Questioning History: The Cold War.* (Hodder Children's Books, 2003)

Timeline

1783	September	Montgolfier brothers launch hot-air balloon
1903		First flight of manned aircraft by Wright brothers
1941		Sir Frank Whittle invents the jet engine
1945	August	Atomic bombs dropped on Hiroshima and Nagasaki in Japan
1952		World's first jet aeroplane goes into service
1957	4 October	USSR launches *Sputnik 1*
1957	November	USSR launches *Sputnik 2*, with dog on board
1958	January	Launch of US *Explorer 1*
1959		The United States sends monkeys into space
1961	12 April	Yuri Gagarin is the first man in space
1962	February	John Glenn is the first American to orbit the Earth
1962	14 December	*Mariner 2* probe sets off for Venus
1965	March	First spacewalk
1965	July	*Mariner 4* probe sets off for Mars
1967		*Apollo 1* catches fire *Soyuz 1* crashes on re-entry
1969	20 July	*Apollo 11* lands on the Moon
1969	November	*Apollo 12* astronauts spend 32 hours on Moon
1971		*Soyuz 11* cosmonauts die from decompression
1971	February	*Apollo 14* astronauts nearly get lost on lunar highlands
1971	August	*Lunar Rover* used for first time
1972	March	*Pioneer 10* sets off for Jupiter
1972	December	*Apollo 17* is the last manned spacecraft to land on the Moon
1986	January	Space station *Mir* launched *Challenger* space shuttle explodes
1987		A satellite confirms the existence of a hole in ozone layer over the Antarctic
1989	December	End of the Cold War
1990		Hubble Space Telescope launched
1991		Helen Sharman, the first British woman in space, visits *Mir* space station.
1999		Satellite *Ikonos* sends back highly detailed pictures of Earth
2001		First space tourist, Dennis Tito
2003		*Colombia* shuttle disintegrates on re-entry, seven killed
2004		NASA rover explores surface of Mars

Glossary

atmosphere	layer of gases surrounding Earth or other plant
atomic bomb	weapon that gets its explosive force from the splitting of atoms of a substance such as uranium or plutonium
Cold War	dispute between the West and Eastern Europe after World War II
command module	main part of the spacecraft that stayed above the Moon, when during Moon landings the lunar module separated from it to descend to the Moon's surface
communist	person or state that follows communism, which is a system of government in which land and industry are owned by the state, and profits are used for the good of the people, but personal freedom and enterprise are limited
cosmonaut	Soviet astronaut
decompression sickness	painful medical condition when nitrogen bubbles form in the blood as a result of rapid changes in pressure
democractic	system of government where leaders are elected by the people
gravity	force exerted by a large object such as a planet, which pulls smaller objects towards it
ICBM	Inter-Continental Ballistic Missile – nuclear missile that can travel from one continent to another
jet engine	powerful engine using gas to thrust it forward
lunar module	part of the spacecraft that separated from the command module to carry the astronauts to the surface of the Moon
nuclear bomb	bomb that gets its explosive force from the joining of atoms of hydrogen and helium, which are two gases
orbit	circle around a planet above its atmosphere
ozone layer	layer of gas in the Earth's atmosphere that reduces the strong effects of the Sun's radiation
probe	unmanned spacecraft sent to find out about other regions of space
re-entry	when a spacecraft comes back into the Earth's atmosphere from space
rocket	engine that pushes gases out behind it
satellite	small object sent into orbit around a planet
solar system	system where planets move in orbit around a sun
Soviet Union	former collection of states in Eastern Europe, led by Russia
space station	spacecraft "parked" in space to act as a base
spacewalk	when an astronaut leaves the spacecraft to go into space
spin-offs	products developed as a result of technological developments
superpowers	name given to the United States and Soviet Union after World War II
weightlessness	being in a place where there is no gravity, so nothing keeps you on the ground and you float in space freely

Index